Contents

Introduction

A handbag can make a statement as well as being a practical means of carrying your essential possessions. Vintage is a key look from couture to high street, and vintage bags are the perfect way to bring that touch of feminine style and retro glamour to any outfit.

Here are eight original projects inspired by the elegance and sophistication of styles from the 1920s to the 1950s. The bags are made from easily acquired materials using straightforward techniques and come in a range of beautiful shapes that give them a really stunning and unique look. All the projects can be created from small amounts of fabric, so will give you that individual designer look without paying designer prices. They make wonderful unique gifts, or you can make them all for yourself; because as every girl knows, you can never have too many bags!

Clara

1920s TWO-TONE ART DECO POCKET BAG

This bag draws inspiration from the flat, simple shape of the beaded cloth and mesh purses of the early 1920s. The long geometric silhouette and panelled appliqué also echo the Art Deco styling of the period.

The handbag as we know it today has only been in existence for a relatively short period. Before this, ladies carried only the bare essentials in small pocket-style reticules. This bag is just large enough to house the modern-day essentials, and the decorative beaded handles are practical for slipping over the wrist, making this an ideal bag for evening wear.

DIMENSIONS

Approximately 9in (23cm) deep by 9in (23cm) wide (excluding the handles)

PATTERN PIECES

 page 34

SUGGESTED FABRICS

For main bag fabric:
cotton-backed fake suede or velveteen (which can be ironed)

For bag lining:
firm-weight plain or patterned silks

For appliqué:
silk brocade and velvet ribbon

YOU WILL NEED

* 14in (36cm) of fake suede for main bag, 36in (92cm) wide
* 14in (36cm) of firm-weight iron-on interfacing, 36in (92cm) wide
* 14in (36cm) of firm-weight silk fabric for lining, 36in (92cm) wide
* 6 x 12in (15 x 31cm) square of patterned silk brocade for appliqué strip
* 6 x 12in (15 x 31cm) square of fusible web for appliqué
* Piece of ¾in (18mm) wide ribbon, 24in (62cm) long, for edging appliqué
* Two pieces x 1½in (4cm) square of craft interfacing (for snap stabilizers)
* One magnetic snap set
* 28in (72cm) of hobby wire for handles in 1.2mm or 16 gauge
* Approximately 36 oval wooden beads (with large holes) size 8 x 16mm (18 per handle)

CUTTING OUT

* Cut 2 x piece **1** (front/back) from main fabric
* Cut 2 x piece **1** (front/back) from iron-on interfacing
* Cut 2 x piece **1** (front/back) from lining fabric
* Cut 1 x piece **2** (appliqué strip) from patterned brocade
* Cut 1 x piece **2** (appliqué strip) from fusible web
* Cut 2 x piece **3** (handle carrier) from main fabric
* Cut 2 x piece **3** (handle carrier) from fusible web
* Cut 2 lengths of ribbon, 12in (31cm) long

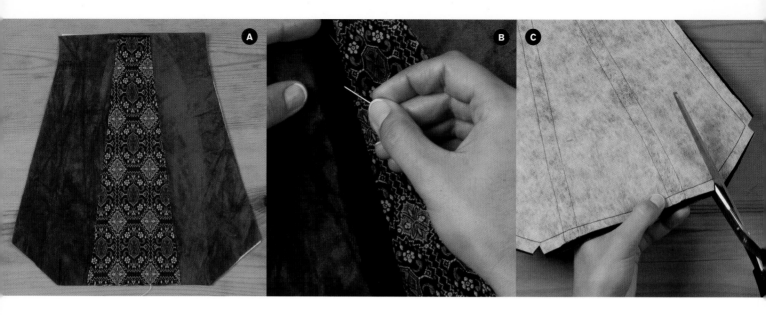

Step 1

Cut the wire coil in two and make a pair of beaded ring handles, using 18 beads per handle. Refer to **beaded ring handles**, on facing page.

Step 2

Iron interfacing pieces **1** to corresponding front and back sections **1** following manufacturer's guidelines.

Step 3

Iron fusible web piece **2** onto appliqué strip piece **2**. Remove paper backing, position appliqué right side up centrally, on right side of front bag piece (following marking lines on pattern) and fuse into place through a cloth (**A**). Pin a strip of velvet ribbon down each side of appliqué (**B**), covering the raw edges of the central appliqué strip on both sides. Stitch in place down both edges of each ribbon strip. Press lightly from the wrong side using a damp cloth.

Step 4

Pin the two interfaced front/back pieces together, right sides together. Stitch around side and lower edges, leaving a ½in (13mm) seam allowance. Clip seam allowance at corners (**C**) and turn right side out.

Step 5

Iron fusible web onto wrong sides of both handle carrier pieces **3**. Peel off paper backing, turn in edges marked with a dotted line on pattern piece to centre and fuse in place.

Step 6

Fold a handle carrier around each beaded ring handle (**D**) and machine-baste along the bottom edge, about ½in (13mm) from raw edges. Secure each handle in place by making a few hand-stitches either side of each handle carrier. Ensure that the stitches are tight up against the beads to stop the handles from sliding round and showing the join in the wire.

Step 7

Pin one handle carrier to the bag front and one to the back centrally (**E**) and machine-baste to bag over the previous row of basting.

Step 8

Transfer magnetic snap placement markers onto the front and back lining pieces **1**, and fix magnetic snap. Remember to use a snap stabilizer as the snaps are fixed to the lining fabric and this will need extra support. Also, if you are using a label, it is at this point that you should stitch it to the back lining of the bag.

Step 9

Stitch lining pieces together around sides and lower edges, but leave a gap of around 5in (13cm). **NB: The hole must be big enough for you to get the handles through!**

Step 10

With right sides together, pin the lining to the bag through all thicknesses (including handle carriers) ensuring that the upper edges are even (**F**). Stitch slowly and carefully through all thicknesses using a medium stitch length and leaving a seam allowance of ½in (13mm). Clip into the seam allowance round the side seams.

Step 11

Turn the bag right side out through the opening in the bottom of the lining and slip-stitch the opening closed. Turn the lining into the bag.

Step 12

Roll the lining with your fingers so that it is not visible from the outside, pin and hand-baste it in place around upper edge of bag. Top-stitch through all layers, about ½in (13mm) from the top of the bag, using a long stitch length. Do up snap, and then give the bag a final light press.

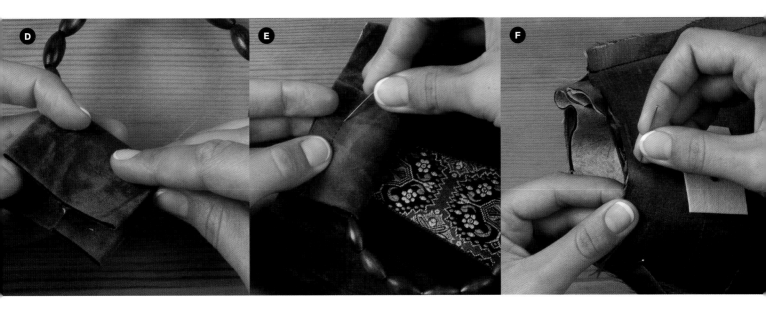

beaded ring handles

To make a beaded ring handle, you will require beads with large centre holes and wire in a heavy weight (gauge). Craft wire can be sized either by gauge or in millimetres. The wire used to make the handles in this book is 16 gauge, or 1.2mm.

To make one handle, around 4in (10cm) in diameter, you will need approximately 14in (36cm) of wire and 26 wooden beads (size 8 to 10mm or larger, with large central holes). If you use longer or larger beads, you must adjust the quantity accordingly.

Step 1

The wire usually comes in a rounded loop, so you will not have to shape it. Cut a loop of wire the size of the handle you require, plus 2–3in (6–8cm). At one end of the loop, using pliers, turn up about 1in (25mm) (**A**).

Step 2

Thread on the beads until you have a handle the size you require, and then turn a bend in the wire directly after the last bead (**B**).

Step 3

Cut ends back to around 1in (25mm) each end, then twist together using pliers (**C**). The ring handle is attached to the bag front or back by means of a 'handle carrier'. This is a short, wider strip of fabric with long edges folded in to the centre and fused using fusible web. The finished strip is then folded around the handle and stitched to the bag before assembly. The join in the wire will not be seen as it will be inside the handle carrier.

Evelyn

1920s ASYMMETRIC CLUTCH WITH VINTAGE BUTTONS

Instead of tucking the bag under-arm, as you would have in the 1920s, I have added a rope handle to this bag. This allows it to rest on the shoulder and sit comfortably under the arm, making it more practical for modern-day use. I've also trimmed it with a row of vintage buttons – a way of including a little piece of history in your modern vintage bag.

Although these buttons are old, they are not particularly fancy. The fact that they once adorned a cardigan or shirt means that there are several of them, and it is the number of buttons, stitched on at an angle down the flap, which finishes this bag off with a flourish. I've made this bag in a striking piece of English woven silk brocade which makes it ideal for evening wear. It would look equally stylish made up in corduroy for day wear with a self-fabric handle.

DIMENSIONS
Approximately 7in (18cm) deep by 11½in (29cm) wide (excluding the handle)

PATTERN PIECES
4 **5** pages 35–36

SUGGESTED FABRICS
For main bag fabric:
silk brocade
For bag lining:
plain silk (firm weight)

YOU WILL NEED
* 12in (31cm) of main fabric, 54in (140cm) wide
* 18in (46cm) of sew-in craft interfacing, 36in (92cm) wide
* 12in (31cm) of lining fabric, 36in (92cm) wide
* 26in (66cm) of cord/rope for handle
* Five medium-sized vintage buttons for decoration
* Two pieces of craft interfacing (for snap stabilizers) 1½in (4cm) square
* One magnetic snap set

CUTTING OUT
* Cut 2 x piece **4** (front/back) from main fabric
* Cut 2 x piece **4** (front/back) from craft interfacing
* Cut 2 x piece **4** (front/back) from lining fabric
* Cut 2 x piece **5** (flap) from main fabric (cut with wrong sides together)
* Cut 1 x piece **5** (flap) from craft interfacing

Step 1

Pin the front and back ④ sections to corresponding front and back interfacing sections ④ and baste-stitch together.

Step 2

Lay the two flap fabric pieces ⑤ wrong sides together, in front of you with the 'tab' facing towards the right. Take top layer off and lay the interfacing piece ⑤ on top of (the wrong side of) the remaining flap piece. Pin together and stitch all around, ¼in (6mm) from outside edge, securing interfacing to bottom flap piece on all sides. Transfer the magnetic snap position marker onto the interfacing side of the flap and fix the non-magnetic half of the snap.

Step 3

Now pin the remaining flap section to the interfaced flap section, right sides together. Stitch together around curved side/lower edges, leaving a ½in (13mm) seam allowance. Trim away any excess bulk, clip into the seam allowance around curves and turn right sides out. Press flat with a damp cloth, then top-stitch all around using a long stitch length. Press again.

Step 4

Make one interfaced section your bag front. Transfer magnetic snap placement marker onto bag front piece and fix magnetic section.

Step 5

Pin the two interfaced front/back pieces together, right sides of main fabric together. Stitch around sides and lower edges, leaving a ½in (13mm) seam allowance. Trim the seam back to ⅜in (1cm) to cut down on bulk. Insert your finger into one of the bottom corners. Match up seam on bottom and side, pin through all thicknesses and stitch straight across the corner to form a gusset.

Step 6

Repeat this on the opposite corner. Turn bag right sides out and press.

Step 7

Pin the finished flap onto the back of the bag (Ⓐ), right outside of flap against right outside of bag back, with raw edges even. Stitch using a long stitch length, about ½in (13mm) from the edge.

Step 8

On outside, positioned next to flap and centred over side seams with raw edges even, pin cord handle to bag (Ⓑ) and hand-baste in place.

Step 9

Stitch lining pieces together at sides and lower edges, leaving an opening of around 5in (13cm) at centre of lower edge for turning. Insert your finger into one of the bottom corners. Match up seam on bottom and side, pin through all thicknesses and stitch straight across the corner to form a gusset as you did for the main bag pieces. Repeat this on the opposite corner.

Step 10

With right sides together, insert bag into lining. Pin lining to bag and baste together around upper edges. Pin and baste through all thicknesses, including flap and cord handles (C). Stitch through all thicknesses using a normal stitch length, and leaving a little over ½in (13mm) seam allowance. Note that this will be a lot of layers to sew through, so stitch slowly and carefully, especially over the cord. Trim the seam back to ⅜in (1cm) to eliminate bulk. Clip into seam allowance at sides.

Step 11

Turn the bag right side out through the opening in the bottom of the lining and slip-stitch the opening closed. Then turn the lining into the bag.

Step 12

Roll the lining with your fingers so that it is not visible from the outside, pin and hand-baste it in place around upper edge of bag. Top-stitch through all layers, a little over ½in (13mm) from the top of the bag, using a long stitch length and taking extra care when sewing through the bulkier areas (D). Close the flap then give a final light press.

Step 13

Lay out your buttons on the flap. I have stitched my buttons on 1in (25mm) apart, following the diagonal of the flap. Hand-stitch in place when you are happy with your arrangement (E).

SEWING TIP

Decorative rope or cording, which is designed for use in furnishing trims, is ideal as a handle for lightweight bags. The ends tend to fray quite badly, so you should wrap a short length of sticky tape around the cord before cutting it – cut in the centre of the sticky tape. This type of cording is usually available by the yard (metre) from the furnishing/upholstery department of fabric and haberdashery shops. Some have short length 'off-cuts' that are not long enough for furnishing trims, but which make perfect bag handles.

Doris

1930s TIE HANDLE BAG WITH ROSE CORSAGE

This bag is based on a shape I found in a late 1930s mail-order catalogue, billed as 'the new over-arm bag'. It features pretty tie handles that give the impression of a large, soft bow. I've changed the shape, extended the handles and added magnetic closures to bring the bag up to date.

Although this floral fabric is retro and fancy enough in its own right, I've added a detachable rose corsage, made from ribbon matched to shades in the print. The vintage-style corsage can also be worn on a cardigan or jacket to tie in with the bag. This is a truly 1930s-inspired project.

DIMENSIONS
Approximately 9½in (24cm) deep by 10½in (27cm) wide (excluding the handle)

PATTERN PIECES
6 **7** **8** pages 37–38

SUGGESTED FABRICS
For main bag fabric:
floral printed cotton (medium weight)
For bag lining:
quilted lining fabric

YOU WILL NEED
* 20in (51cm) of main fabric, 48in (122cm) wide
* 14in (36cm) of lining fabric, 36in (92cm) wide
* 14in (36cm) of wadding, 36in (92cm) wide
* Two pieces of craft interfacing (for snap stabilizers) 1½in (4cm) square
* One magnetic snap set
* One piece of plastic canvas to insert in base 8¼ x 2in (21 x 6cm)

CUTTING OUT
* Cut 2 x piece **6** (front/back) from main fabric on fold
* Cut 2 x piece **7** (handle) from main fabric on fold
* Cut 2 x piece **8** (front/back lining) from wadding on fold
* Cut 2 x piece **8** (front/back lining) from quilted lining fabric on fold

Step 1

Transfer pleat lines from pattern template using tailor's tacks. Make pleats on front and back pieces **6** by bringing markers together on right side of fabric to form pleats. Press pleats towards outer edges of bag on wrong side (**A**).

Step 2

Pin front and back sections to corresponding front and back wadding sections **8** and machine-baste together (**B**).

Step 3

Transfer * marks from pattern template onto front and back pieces using tailor's tacks. Pin the two front/back pieces together, right sides of main fabric together. Stitch together at side and lower edges between * marks, leaving corners free (**C**). Back-stitch at * marks as reinforcement. Fold the lower corners of the bag matching seams, and stitch straight across to form gusset.

Step 4

Make tie handles by folding each handle section **7** in half lengthways along fold line, with wrong sides together. Stitch down open sides leaving straight end open for turning.

Step 5

Pin handles to front and back sections, centring over pleats and with raw edges even. The points on the ties should face in opposite directions. Baste in place (**D**).

Step 6

Attach magnetic snap to each side of lining at position marked on pattern piece.

Step 7

Transfer * marks from pattern template onto front and back lining pieces using tailor's tacks. Pin the two front/back lining pieces together, right sides of main fabric together. Stitch together at side and lower edges between * marks, leaving corners free and leaving a gap of about 5in (13cm) for turning. Back-stitch at * marks to reinforce. Fold the lower corners of the bag matching seams, and stitch straight across in order to form a gusset.

Step 8

With the bag right side out, insert it into the lining. Pin with raw edges even on each side of the bag, with * marks matched (**E**). Stitch between * marks either side of the bag, around side and upper edges (the handles will be sandwiched between). Make a few back-stitches at * marks as reinforcement. Clip corners and clip carefully into side seams at * marks.

Step 9

Turn the bag right side out through the opening. Push upper corners outwards. Insert plastic canvas into bottom of bag through opening in lining. Slip-stitch opening closed and insert lining into bag. Press top edges and bag thoroughly.

To make the matching corsage

YOU WILL NEED
* 36in (92cm) of grosgrain ribbon 1½in (4cm) wide
* 14in (36cm) of grosgrain ribbon 1in (2.5cm) wide for leaves
* brooch backing bar (with holes for stitching)

Step 1
Make a folded rose using the wide grosgrain ribbon. Refer to **ribbon roses**, right. Make two leaves using the narrower grosgrain ribbon, by folding and stitching as shown in picture (**F**), and hand-stitching to back of rose (**G**), covering any raw edges.

Step 2
Hand-stitch a brooch bar to the back of the corsage (**H**) and pin onto the left side of the bag front.

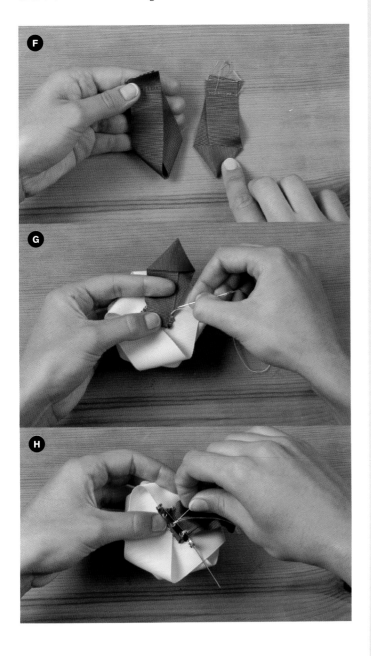

ribbon roses

This bag is trimmed with a ribbon rose, made using the 'twist and fold' method. It took me some time to get the hang of this, but perseverance is well worthwhile as there are so many bags which can be brought to life with blooms of this kind. They can also double as corsage brooches, and as there are so many beautiful ribbons on the market (including some vintage), there is no limit to the variations you can make.

Step1
Take a length of 1½in (38mm) width ribbon approximately 32in (82cm) long. Roll one end over about three or four times to form a centre. Hand-stitch through all layers at the base of the rose (**A**).

Step 2
The ribbon must then be twisted spirally and secured with stitches at the base each time it is folded. Make certain that you sew through all of the layers each time, to ensure that the folds are firmly fixed in place (**B**).

Step 3
Once a rose of the required size is achieved, cut off remaining ribbon, fold the raw edge under and stitch in place (**C**), (**D**).

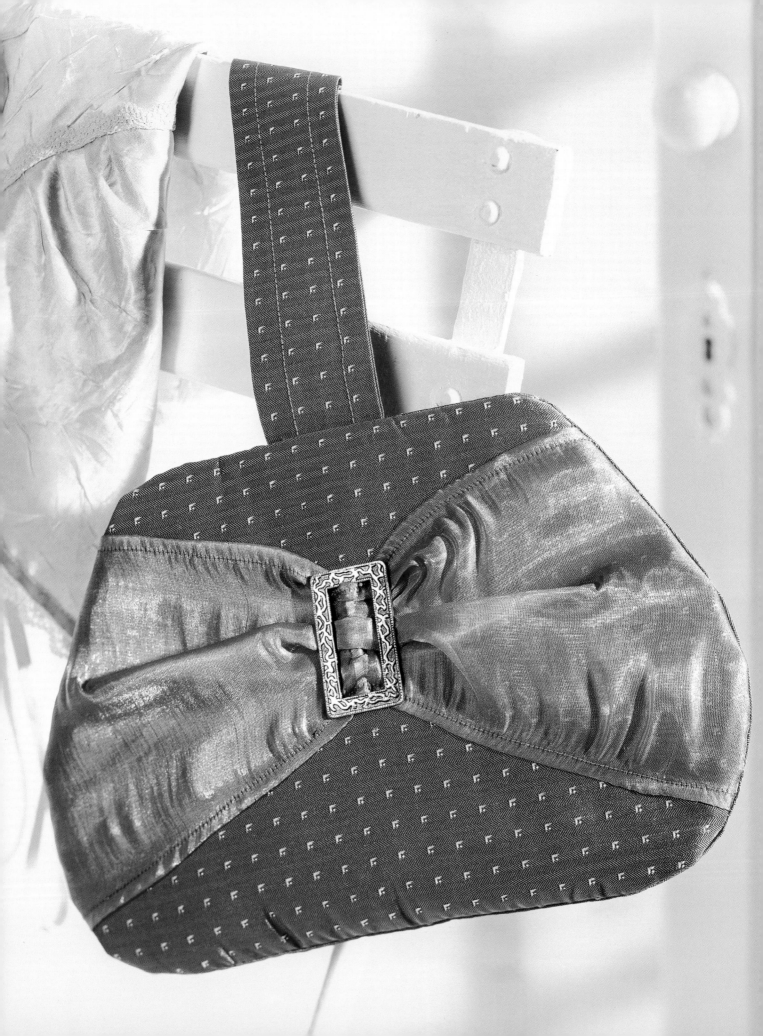

Lois

1930s BAG WITH DRAPED BUCKLE TRIM

This bag is delightfully dressy in style and features an antique metal buckle, attached with a swathe of sheer fabric. It still has the characteristic flat styling of the early 1930s clutch, but I've added a wrist strap for ease of use.

DIMENSIONS
Approximately 7½in (19cm) deep by 10½in (27cm) wide (excluding the handle)

PATTERN PIECES
9 **10** **11** page 39

SUGGESTED FABRICS
For main bag fabric:
firm-weight woven silk brocade
For bag lining:
plain or patterned silk
For the swathe:
sheer fabric, with two-tone finish if possible

I first saw a simple and appealing bag with this silhouette in an original late 1930s mail-order catalogue and thought it would make a great shape for embellishment. For this project I've used a smart woven English silk fabric for the main body and added the shot silk drape to give the front an extra dimension. The drape is caught in the centre with a decorative buckle. Using a vintage buckle is an excellent way of combining a piece of the past in your modern handbag.

YOU WILL NEED
* 18in (46cm) of main fabric, 36in (92cm) wide
* 8in x 16in (21 x 41cm) of sheer fabric for drape trim
* 12in (31cm) of lining fabric, 36in (92cm) wide
* 12 x 14in (31 x 36cm) of sew-in craft interfacing
* 12 x 14in (31 x 36cm) of wadding
* 12 x 14in (31 x 36cm) of iron-on interfacing
* 18in (46cm) of grosgrain ribbon for handle backing, approximately 1in (25mm) wide
* Piece of fusible web 4 x 18in (10 x 46cm) for handle
* Zip fastener, 7in (18cm) length
* Vintage-style buckle, approximately 2in (6cm) deep

CUTTING OUT
* Cut 2 x piece **9** (front/back) from main fabric
* Cut 2 x piece **9** (front/back) from lining fabric
* Cut 1 x piece **9** (front/back) from iron-on interfacing
* Cut 1 x piece **9** (front/back) from craft interfacing
* Cut 1 x piece **9** (front/back) from wadding
* Cut 1 x piece **10** (front drape overlay) from sheer fabric on fold
* Cut 1 x piece **11** (handle) from main fabric and fusible web on fold

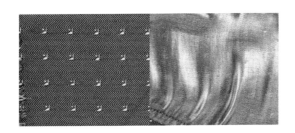

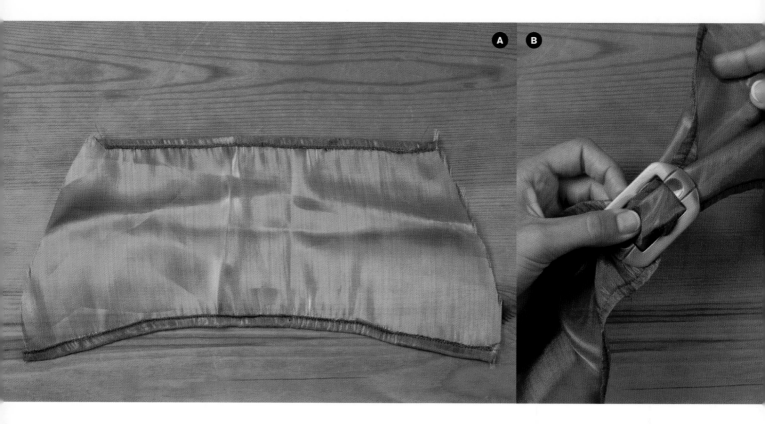

Step 1

Pin front piece **9** to wadding and then back with craft interfacing **9** piece. The wadding will be sandwiched between the fabric and the interfacing. Machine-baste all layers together around outside edge.

Step 2

Machine-neaten top and bottom edges of front drape overlay **10** by stitching over the edges using a close and narrow zigzag stitch (**A**). This will prevent fraying. After neatening, turn over a small hem and top-stitch about ¼in (6mm) from each edge. Thread the drape through the buckle and position centrally, arranging gathers evenly (**B**).

Step 3

Pin drape in place on front between positions marked on pattern piece (**C**). Raw edges of drape should be even with side edges of bag front. Stitch in place ¼in (6mm) from the edge. From wrong side of front, hand-stitch through to right side and secure drape in place at several points along buckle (**D**).

Step 4

Iron fusible web onto reverse of handle **11**, peel off paper backing, turn in long edges to centre and fuse in place. Stitch strip of grosgrain ribbon centrally over join. Baste the raw edges of the handle together at bottom edge, with fabric side out.

Step 5

Pin the handle to the bag front piece, centring over centre front, and machine-baste to bag over the previous row of basting (**E**).

Step 6

Iron interfacing onto back piece. Pin back piece to back lining piece, mark zip placement onto interfacing side of back and set zipper in. Remember to leave the zipper open after setting in, as you will turn the bag through this.

Step 7

Pin the interfaced front and back sections together, right sides of main fabric together. Stitch right around entire outside edge, through main bag pieces, including handle, leaving a ½in (13mm) seam allowance. Leave the lining piece free. Clip into the seam allowance at intervals around curved edges.

Step 8

Pin the remaining lining piece to the back lining (which is now attached to the back via the zip) and stitch pieces together around entire outside edge, leaving an opening of around 5in (13cm) at centre of lower edge for turning.

Step 9

Turn the bag right side out, first through the opening in the bottom of the lining and then through the zipper. Push curved edges outwards. Slip-stitch the opening in lining closed. Turn the lining into the bag; do up zipper and press bag lightly.

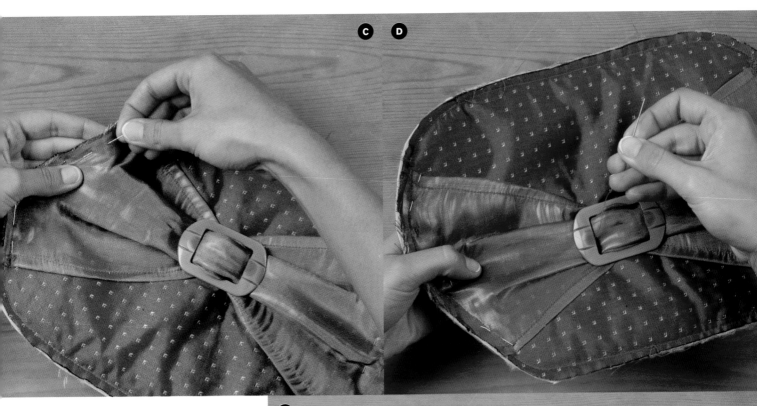

C   D

E

VARIATION

You may be lucky enough to find an interesting buckle on an old garment at home. If not, it's possible to stumble upon some real treasures in thrift stores or remnant shops, often for very little cost.

If you can't find a metal buckle, a Bakelite or plastic one will suffice, and as these come in very pretty colours, you could consider making this project entirely from printed floral cottons, making it a perfect day bag.

Rita

1930s PLEAT BAG WITH SILK ROSE TRIM

This bag is a development of the previous project (Lois).
It features pleat detailing on the front and is trimmed with a silk
fabric rose and leaves, stitched at an angle. The pleats are characteristic
of styles of the 1930s, but making the bag in a plain cotton
twill fabric updates it for modern use.

The spotted silk trimming and light colouring of this bag give it a dressy appearance while still being summery, making it ideal for a wedding or garden party. If you don't want such a formal piece, you could always use a polka dot or candy-striped cotton for the trim instead.

DIMENSIONS
Approximately 7½in (19cm) deep
by 10½in (27cm) wide (excluding
the handle)

PATTERN PIECES
12 **13** **14** **15** **16** pages 39–41

SUGGESTED FABRICS
For main bag fabric:
medium-weight cottons (twill, etc)
For bag lining:
plain or quilted cotton
For the rose and leaf:
polka dot and plain silk

YOU WILL NEED
* 18in (46cm) of main fabric, 48in (122cm) wide
* 12in (31cm) of lining fabric, 36in (92cm) wide
* 12 x 14in (31 x 36cm) of sew-in craft interfacing
* 12 x 14in (31 x 36cm) of iron-on interfacing
* 18in (46cm) of velvet ribbon for handle trim approx 1½in (38mm) wide
* One piece of fusible web 18 x 4in (46 x 10cm) for handle
* Zip fastener, 7in (18cm) length
* Two squares of silk for leaves – 6 x 6in (15 x 15cm) exactly
* 22 x 4in (56 x 10cm) of polka dot silk for rose

CUTTING OUT
* Cut 1 x piece **12** (front) from main fabric on fold
* Cut 1 x piece **13** (back) from main fabric
* Cut 2 x piece **13** (back) from lining fabric
* Cut 1 x piece **13** (back) from iron-on interfacing
* Cut 1 x piece **13** (back) from sew-in craft interfacing
* Cut 1 x piece **14** (handle) from main fabric and fusible web on fold
* Cut 1 x piece **15** fabric rose from spotted silk on fold
* Cut 2 x piece **16** fabric leaf from plain silk

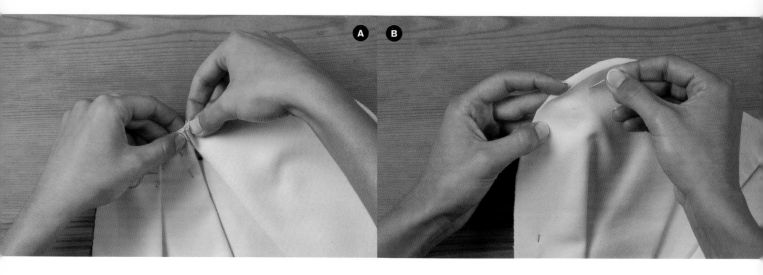

Step 1

Transfer markings for front pleats onto bag front, using tailor's tacks. Make pleats in bag front by bringing markers together on right side of fabric to form pleats. Press pleats towards outer edges of bag on wrong side (**A**). **NB: Pleats will meet in the middle on the right side of the bag and the side pleats will overlap the centre pleats on the wrong side (follow directions on pattern piece).** Baste pleats in place at top and bottom edge of bag.

Step 2

Pin front piece **12** to craft interfacing **13** piece (**B**). Machine-baste together around entire outside edge.

Step 3

Iron fusible web onto reverse of handle **14**, peel off paper backing, turn in long edges to centre and fuse in place. Stitch strip of velvet ribbon centrally over join. Baste raw edges of handle together at bottom, having velvet ribbon side out.

Step 4

Pin the handle to the bag front piece, centring over centre front, and machine-baste to bag over the previous row of basting.

Step 5

Iron interfacing onto back piece. Pin the back piece to the back lining piece, mark zip placement onto interfacing side of back and set zipper in. Remember to leave the zipper **open** after setting in, as you will turn the bag through this.

Step 6

Pin the interfaced front and back sections together, right sides of main fabric together. Stitch front and back together around entire outside edge, including handle, but leaving the lining piece free. Stitch with a ½in (13mm) seam allowance. Clip into the seam allowance at intervals around curved edges.

Step 7

Pin the remaining lining piece to the back lining (which is now attached to the back via the zip) and stitch pieces together around entire outside edge, leaving an opening of around 5in (13cm) at centre of lower edge for turning.

Step 8

Turn the bag right side out, first through the opening in the bottom of the lining and then through the zipper. Push curved edges outwards. Slip-stitch the opening in lining closed. Turn the lining into the bag; do up zipper, and then press the bag using a cloth.

Step 9

Make a fabric rose from the polka dot silk. Fold the rose **15** piece in half lengthways and press. Machine stitch curved long raw edges together approximately ¼in (6mm) from raw edge. Run a gathering stitch along the previous row of stitches and pull gathers up (**C**). Coil into a flower shape and secure with hand-stitches at the back (**D**).

Step 10

Cut two leaf **16** pieces from the plain silk. Fold one square in half diagonally, then fold in half again (**E**). Stitch together along bottom raw edges, then machine neaten using a zigzag stitch. Run a gathering stitch along the previous row of stitching and pull gathers up (**F**). Fold gathers in half evenly and stitch a seam along the gathered edges (**G**).

Step 11

Hand-stitch leaves together at an angle, then stitch the rose on top of the leaves. Make sure that all rough edges are covered.

Step 12

Stitch rose and leaves to bag at centre point, with leaves facing to the left at an angle.

VARIATIONS

Because of the small amount of silk required to make the rose and leaf trim for this bag, and as it will be used purely decoratively, you could consider using vintage scarves, hankies or other small pieces of vintage textile. More modern 'retro' scarves can also provide a source of interesting silk fabric – you can often pick these up in charity shops or thrift stores.

Patricia

1940s AUTUMN BOW CRESCENT BAG

This inventive crescent shape recurs quite frequently in home sewing pattern catalogues throughout the 1940s. I've seen it with various methods of fastening, but through experimenting have found that using a handle that threads through a loop at the other end is by far the most convenient for modern use.

It looks small and neat when done up, but this is actually quite a roomy little bag. It uses wadding as a means of bulking without stiffening, which is essential, as this bag relies on being soft enough to fold into its wonderful 'croissant' shape. Made in this hard-wearing wool tweed, I felt the bag could benefit from a contrasting 'statement' trim, and that's why I decided on this soft, foppish velvet bow. The colour choice has also added to the period feel of this piece.

DIMENSIONS
Approximately 7in (18cm) deep by 11in (28cm) wide, when opened out

PATTERN PIECES
17 **18** **19** **20** **21** pages 42–43

SUGGESTED FABRICS
For main bag fabric:
wool tweed or flannel (firm weight)
For bag lining:
plain/patterned silk, cotton prints
For the bow:
soft drapey velvet

YOU WILL NEED
* 17in (44cm) of main fabric, minimum 36in (92cm) wide
* 12in x 36in (31 x 92cm) of lining fabric
* 12in x 36in (31 x 92cm) of wadding
* 9 x 30in (23 x 77cm) of velvet for bow
* One piece of fusible web 3 x 6in (8 x 15cm) for bow centre and loop fastener
* Zip fastener, 7in (18cm) length
* 17 x 10in (44 x 26cm) of iron-on interfacing for handle stiffener

CUTTING OUT
* Cut 2 x piece **17** (front/back) from main fabric
* Cut 2 x piece **17** (front/back) from lining fabric
* Cut 2 x piece **17** (front/back) from wadding
* Cut 2 x piece **18** (handle) from main fabric and iron-on interfacing
* Cut 1 x piece **19** (loop fastener) from main fabric and fusible web
* Cut 2 x piece **20** (main bow piece) from velvet
* Cut 1 x piece **21** (bow centre) from velvet and fusible web

Step 1

Pin front and back pieces **17** to corresponding wadding pieces. Baste together around outside edge.

Step 2

Transfer * marks from pattern template using tailor's tacks. Stitch front and back sections together at upper edges, leaving open between *. Baste the section between the * marks and press the seam open flat.

Step 3

With the zipper closed and face down, centre it over the basted pressed seam and baste in place approx ¼in (6mm) from the teeth of the zipper. You will use this basting line as a sewing guide from the other side. Turn bag right side up and from right side, machine stitch zipper in place. Stitch over basting and across top and bottom ends of zipper. You will need to use a zipper foot for this. Take out basting stitches and leave the zipper open.

Step 4

Pin and stitch front and back **17** sections together around curved edge (leaving upper corners free).

Step 5

Make handle. Iron interfacing onto the reverse of both handle pieces **18**. Pin handle pieces right sides together and stitch down each long edge, leaving short ends open (**A**). Clip curved seam allowance and turn handle right side out. Press and top-stitch about ½in (13mm) from each long edge. Baste ends together flat (**B**).

Step 6

Make loop fastener by ironing fusible web to the reverse of piece **19**, folding long edges to centre and fusing in place. Fold in half lengthways again and stitch open long edges together, approximately ¼in (6mm) from the edge.

Step 7

On outside, at one end, pin and baste handle to upper side (corner) edges of front and back, centring over seam. At other end, pin and baste loop fastener (ends of loop should be 1in/25mm apart) (**C**).

Step 8

From the **inside**, fold the upper corners, matching seams and stitch straight across, through handle/loop fastener (**D**).

Step 9

Make lining. Stitch front and back lining sections together at upper edges, leaving open between *. Press open the seam allowance for 'open' section. Stitch front and back right sides together around curved edge, leaving upper corners free. From the inside, fold the upper corners, matching seams and stitch straight across.

Step 10

Turn bag inside out and insert into lining, wrong sides together. Pin the pressed edge of the lining to the zipper tape and hand slip-stitch in place (**E**).

Step 11

Construct the bow. Refer to **making an angled bow**, right.

Step 12

Hand-stitch bow in place at loop end of bag, centring over side seam (**F**).

making an angled bow

This is a floppy style of bow with angled corners. You will need two pattern pieces – main bow and bow centre. Cut two main bow pieces and one bow centre piece from your chosen bow fabric.

Step 1
Pin two main bow pieces right sides together. Stitch around the outside edge, leaving an opening between * and *, for turning the bow to the right side. Use a seam allowance of ½in (13mm) (A).

Step 2
Trim seams back to ¼in (6mm), clip corners and turn right side out. Hand slip-stitch opening closed (B).

Step 3
Gather or pleat along centre line of bow using large hand-gathering stitches. Pull up gathers/pleats and secure with several overhand stitches (C).

Step 4
Iron fusible web to wrong side of bow centre piece. Peel off paper backing, turn long edges of piece in so that they meet in the middle, then press with a cloth (D).

Step 5
Stitch short ends together to form a short tube and turn the tube right side out (E).

Step 6
Slide tube over the bow and position it in the middle, covering the gathers (F). Hand tack centre in place from behind.

Shirley

1950s TWO-TONE FLOWER TRIM SMALL BAG

Although this bag is small, it has found its way into the 1950s section because of its nice bucket shape and its flowery trims, which were very popular in this decade.

This bag features contrast side panels, a single wrist strap with contrasting underside and purchased ribbon blooms in a toning shade, backed with handmade leaves. It looks quite dressy, but the simple solid shape, especially when made up in functional tweed and fake suede, makes it a very serviceable day bag, just large enough to house the essentials.

DIMENSIONS

Approximately 7in (18cm) deep by 10in (26cm) wide (excluding the handle)

PATTERN PIECES

22 **23** **24** **25** **26** **27**
pages 44–46

SUGGESTED FABRICS

For main bag fabric:
patterned wool tweed
For contrast panels:
fake suede
For bag lining:
plain or patterned silk

YOU WILL NEED

* 18in (46cm) of tweed fabric, 36in (92cm) wide
* 18in (46cm) of contrast fabric, 18in (46cm) wide for side panels/handle
* 9in (23cm) of lining fabric, 36in (92cm) wide
* 12in (31cm) of heavy-weight sew-in interfacing, 36in (92cm) wide
* Fusible web 7 x 18in (18 x 46cm) for handle
* Two 1½in (4cm) square pieces of craft interfacing (for snap stabilizers)
* One magnetic snap set
* Piece of plastic canvas to insert in base 1½ x 7¾in (4 x 20cm)
* Three purchased ribbon flowers for trim
* Approximately 36in (92cm) of narrow ribbon (¼in/6mm wide) for the leaves

CUTTING OUT

* Cut 1 x piece **22** (front centre panel) from main fabric
* Cut 2 x piece **23** (front side panel) from contrast fabric
* Cut 1 x piece **24** (back) from main fabric
* Cut 2 x piece **24** (back) from interfacing
* Cut 2 x piece **25** (facing) from main fabric
* Cut 2 x piece **26** (front/back lining) from lining fabric
* Cut 1 x piece **27** (handle) from main fabric on fold
* Cut 1 x piece **27** (handle) from contrast fabric on fold
* Cut 2 x piece **27** (handle) from fusible web on fold

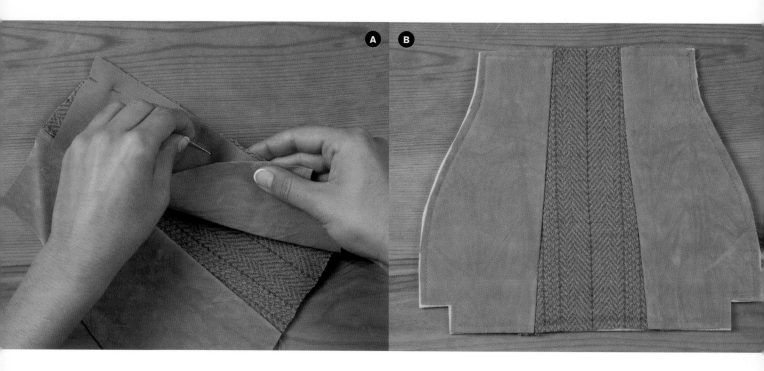

Step 1

Pin front centre panel piece **22** and front side panel pieces **23** together along edges marked with dotted line on pattern templates (**A**). Baste and machine stitch together, leaving a ½in (13mm) seam allowance. Press seams toward outer edges.

Step 2

Pin assembled front piece to one interfacing piece **24** and baste together around outside edges. Machine stitch (using a long stitch length) along the seams of the front panels (**B**).

Step 3

Cut the narrow ribbon into six equal lengths of around 6in (15cm). Make leaves by twisting and folding as in pictures (**C**) and (**D**). You will need two leaves for each flower. Secure folds with a few stitches, then stitch leaves to bag centre front at positions marked with an X on the pattern template. Layer one leaf on top of the other in a cross shape (**E**).

Step 4

Hand-stitch the three ribbon roses down the centre front panel positioned over the leaves (**F**).

Step 5

Pin the back section to the corresponding back interfacing piece and baste-stitch together around outside edges.

Step 6

Pin the two interfaced front/back sections right sides together. Stitch around sides and lower edges, leaving a ½in (13mm) seam allowance, and leaving the corners free. Trim the seams back to ⅜in (1cm) to cut down on bulk. Fold the lower corners of the bag matching seams, and stitch straight across to form gusset.

Step 7

Repeat this on the opposite corner. Turn bag right sides out and press.

Step 8

Make handle by ironing fusible web onto reverse side of both handle pieces **27**. Fold in long edges to centre and fuse in place. Pin handle sections wrong sides together, with folded edges even. Stitch together down both long edges approximately ¼in (6mm) from the edge.

Step 9

On outside of bag, position handle at centre front and centre back. With raw edges even, pin handle to bag and baste in place. Note that you will have to take the handle under the bag and the bag will need to be folded up slightly whilst sewing.

Step 10

Stitch lower edges of facing pieces **25** to upper edges of lining pieces **26** with right sides together.

Step 11

On facing pieces **25**, transfer snap marker positions and fix magnetic snaps using stabilizer interfacing squares.

Step 12

Stitch lining/facing pieces together at side and lower edges, leaving corners free and leaving a gap of around 5in (13cm) in the centre of the bottom for turning the bag through. Fold the lower corners of the lining matching seams, and stitch straight across to form gusset as you did for main bag.

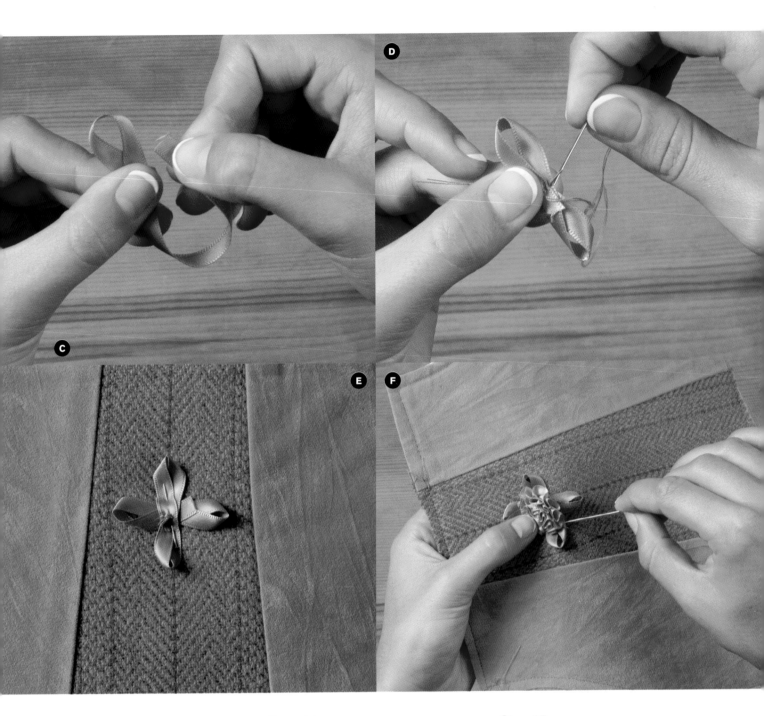

Step 13

With right sides together, pin lining to bag with raw edges even, and baste together around upper edges. Pin and baste through all thicknesses, including handle. Stitch using a medium stitch length and leaving a ½in (13mm) seam allowance. As this is a small bag with a narrow 'neck', this stage can be tricky, so stitch slowly and carefully, especially over the handle. Trim the seam back to around ⅜in (1cm) to eliminate bulk and clip into the seam allowance near side seams.

Step 14

Turn the bag right side out through the opening in the lining. Insert plastic canvas into base, then slip-stitch the opening closed. Turn the lining into the bag.

Step 15

Roll the facing with your fingers so that it is not visible from the outside, pin and hand-baste it in place round upper edge of bag. Top-stitch through all layers, about ½in (13mm) from the top of the bag, using a medium to long stitch length. The bag is small and quite tricky to access for top-stitching, so take extra care when sewing through the bulkier areas. Close the bag and then give it a press.

Gloria

1950s PICTURE BAG WITH ROPE HANDLE

This fun but practical bag combines vintage-look ticking striped cotton, old-fashioned braid buttons, a tassel cord handle and a 1950s' feel photo appliqué. You can personalize it with any picture you like, but I've chosen an image of a Victorian boot.

DIMENSIONS
Approximately 14in (36cm) deep by 15½in (39cm) wide (excluding the handle)

PATTERN PIECES
28 **29** **30** pages 47–48

SUGGESTED FABRICS
For main bag fabric:
medium-weight ticking striped fabric
For bag lining:
quilted cotton lining fabric

Photo image bags have become extremely popular and offer a great way to personalize your accessories. The black braid trim around the picture gives the impression of a frame and the tiny roses at each corner lend a feminine finishing touch. The choice of almost monochromatic shades also adds to the vintage feel.

YOU WILL NEED
* 20in (51cm) of main fabric, 54in (140cm) wide
* 20in (51cm) of firm-weight sew-in interfacing, 48in (122cm) wide
* 18in (46cm) of quilted lining fabric, 48in (122cm) wide
* 9in (23cm) zipper
* Piece of plastic canvas 11½ x 3½in (29 x 9cm) for base
* 7 x 20in (18 x 51cm) of iron-on interfacing for handle carrier tabs
* 60in (154cm) of twisted rope cording for handle
* A cut-out or transfer image in size of your choice printed onto plain cotton fabric
* Approximately 36in (92cm) of gimp braid or ribbon (enough to frame your chosen image)
* Two braid-covered buttons
* Four small ribbon roses

CUTTING OUT
* Cut 2 x piece **28** (front/back) from main fabric on fold
* Cut 2 x piece **28** (front/back) from sew-in interfacing on fold
* Cut 2 x piece **29** (front/back lining) from quilted lining fabric on fold
* Cut 4 x piece **30** (handle carrier tabs) from main fabric
* Cut 4 x piece **30** (handle carrier tabs) from iron-on interfacing

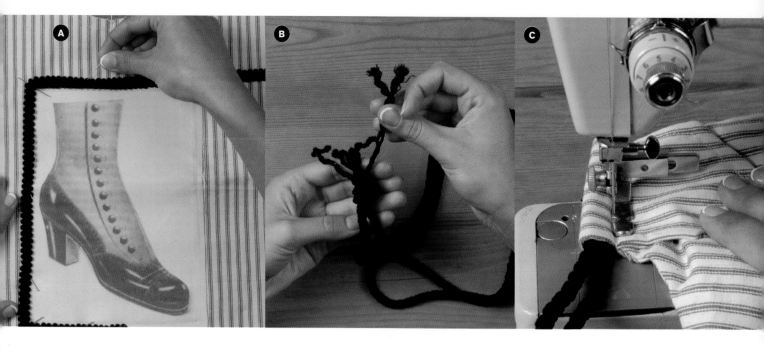

Step 1

Pin the front and back **28** sections to the corresponding front and back **28** interfacing sections and baste-stitch together.

Step 2

Take your image (now printed onto fabric) and position in a central place on the bag front piece. Pin and baste in place, then machine stitch around outside of image about ¼in (6mm) from the edge.

Step 3

Pin braid around image, ensuring that all raw edges are covered (**A**). Starting at the centre bottom of the image, curve braid around the corners and pin diagonally into corners to secure. When you have reached the point where you started, tuck end of braid under to neaten. Baste then stitch both edges of the braid to secure. Hand-stitch a ribbon rose at each corner. **NB: If you are using a 'transfer' image, do not iron the image directly at any stage.**

Step 4

Make handle tabs. Iron interfacing onto reverse side of each tab piece. Place two tab **30** pieces right sides together and stitch round side and bottom edges, leaving top edge open for turning. Clip corners and turn right side out. Top-stitch about ½in (13mm) from the edge. Repeat for other tab.

Step 5

Place tabs on front and stitch in place along top edge.

Step 6

Pin back piece **28** to back lining piece **29**, right sides together, mark zip placement onto reverse interfaced side of back and set zip in. Remember to leave the zipper **open** after setting in, as you will turn the bag through this later.

Step 7

Pin front and back sections right sides together. Stitch right around top and side edges, and along the bottom edge, leaving corners free. Stitch through main bag pieces, including handle carrier tabs, pivoting at corners and leaving a ½in (13mm) seam allowance. Ensure that you leave the lining piece free.

Step 8

Clip curve at top and clip corners. Fold the lower corners of the bag matching seams, and stitch straight across to form gusset. You will have to access the corners through the zipper opening.

Step 9

Pin the remaining front lining piece to the back lining (which is now attached to the back of the bag via the zip) and stitch right around the top and side edges, and along the bottom edge, leaving the corners free and leaving an opening of around 6in (15cm) at centre of lower edge for turning. Fold the lower corners of the bag lining matching seams, and stitch straight across to form gusset.

Step 10

Turn bag right side out, first through the opening in the bottom of the lining and then through the zipper. Push corners outwards, pull tabs upwards, shape curved edges and press top of bag thoroughly. Insert plastic canvas in to base of bag and slip-stitch the opening in lining closed. Turn the lining into the bag; do up zipper and press bag again, avoiding the transfer image.

Step 11

Make the handle. Fold the twisted cord rope in half and tie the cut ends together in a tight overhand knot, approximately 3½in (9cm) from the ends. Untwist and unravel the ends of the rope to form a tassel (**B**).

Step 12

Fold handle carrier tabs over the double thickness of cord rope, gauge the depth of the loops and pin in place either side. The tabs should sit tightly against the rope and the knots need to be big enough so that the handle cannot slip off. Pull the knot up against the left-hand side tab. The folded end of the rope should be hanging from the other side of the right tab. Stitch the tabs in place using a zipper foot (**C**). You should stitch in the seam line from the reverse side of the bag. Tie a knot approximately 3½in (9cm) from the folded end of rope, cut the loop and form a tassel as you did with the other end (**D**, **E**). Pull the second knot close up against the right tab.

Step 13

Stitch a braid-covered button each side of the top of the bag, on the flap part of the handle carriers.

①②③ Clara

Enlarge all pattern pieces by 165%

appliqué
marker

appliqué
marker

snap marker

• •

① Clara
front/back

appliqué
marker

appliqué
marker

when photocopying, align dotted rule with top edge of glass

join edges at dotted lines

③ Clara
handle carrier

join edges at dotted lines

② Clara
appliqué strip

④ Evelyn

Enlarge all pattern pieces by 165%

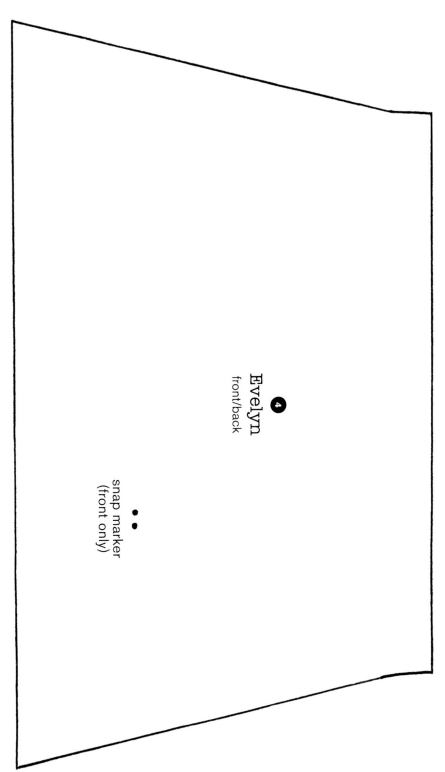

Evelyn
front/back ④

snap marker
(front only)

Enlarge all pattern pieces by 165%

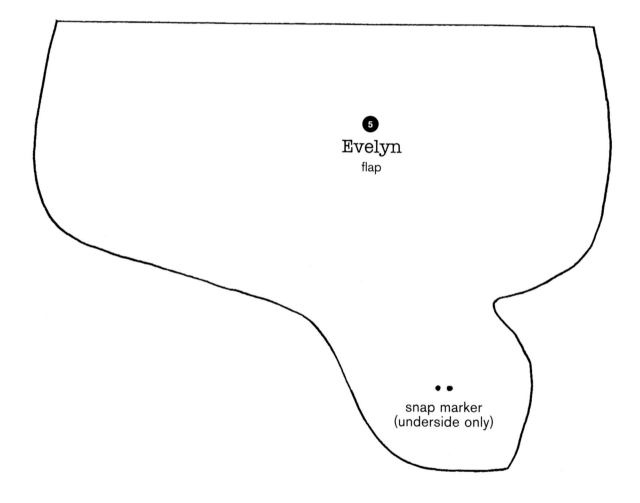

5

Evelyn
flap

snap marker
(underside only)

when photocopying, align dotted rule with top edge of glass

6 7 Doris

Enlarge all pattern pieces by 165%

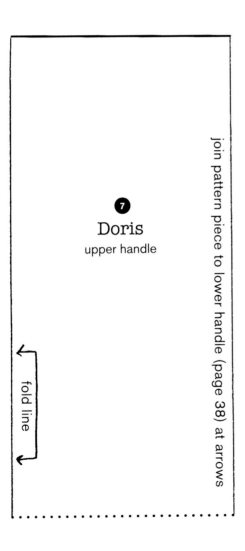

7

Doris
upper handle

fold line

join pattern piece to lower handle (page 38) at arrows

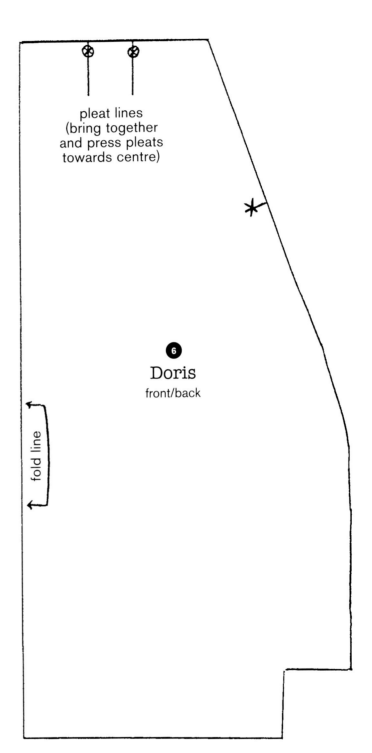

pleat lines
(bring together
and press pleats
towards centre)

6

Doris
front/back

fold line

Enlarge all pattern pieces by 165%

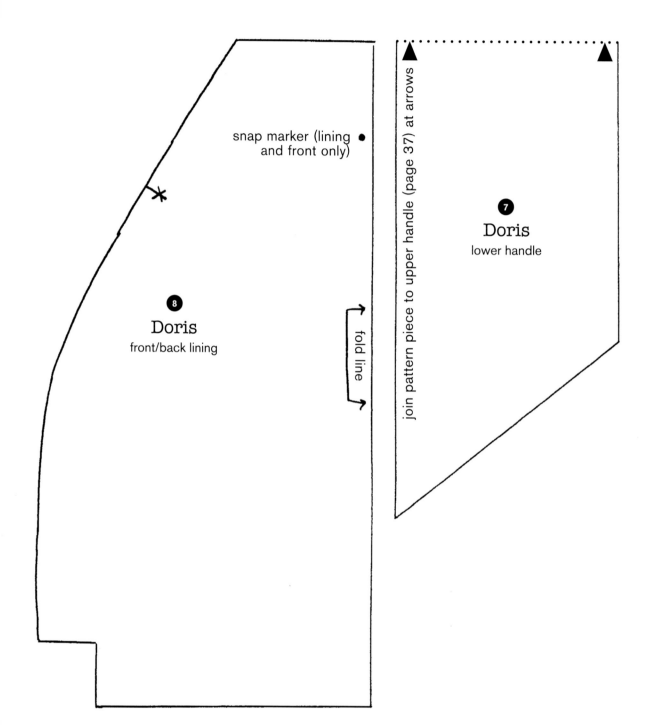

snap marker (lining
and front only) ●

❽
Doris
front/back lining

fold line

join pattern piece to upper handle (page 37) at arrows

❼
Doris
lower handle

when photocopying, align dotted rule with top edge of glass

❾ ❿ ⓫ ⓮ Lois/Rita

Enlarge all pattern pieces by 165%

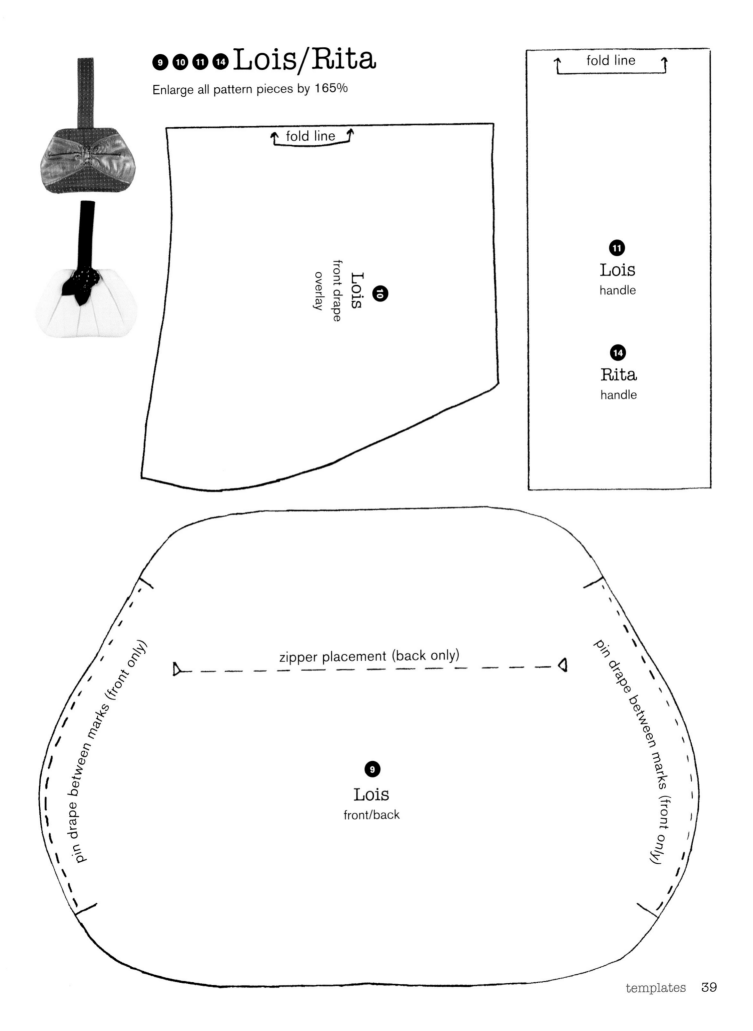

fold line

❿
Lois
front drape
overlay

fold line

⓫
Lois
handle

⓮
Rita
handle

zipper placement (back only)

pin drape between marks (front only)

pin drape between marks (front only)

❾
Lois
front/back

⑫ ⑯ Rita

Enlarge all pattern
pieces by 165%

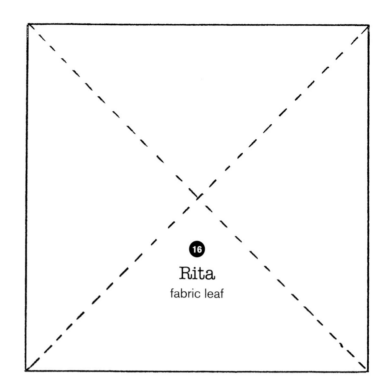

⑯

Rita
fabric leaf

when photocopying, align dotted rule with top edge of glass

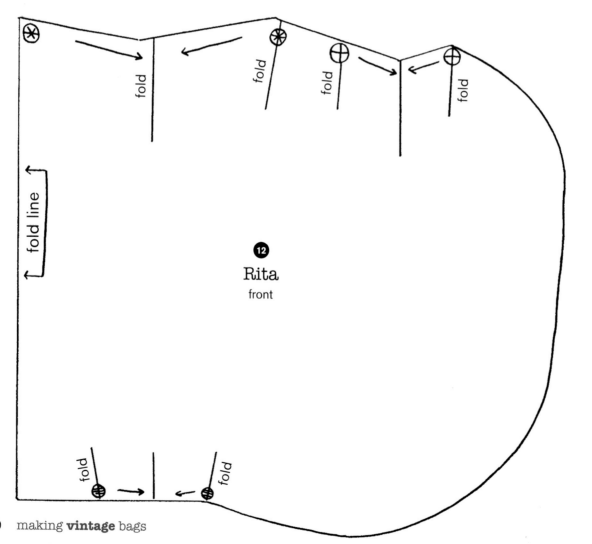

fold

fold

fold

fold

fold line

⑫

Rita
front

fold

fold

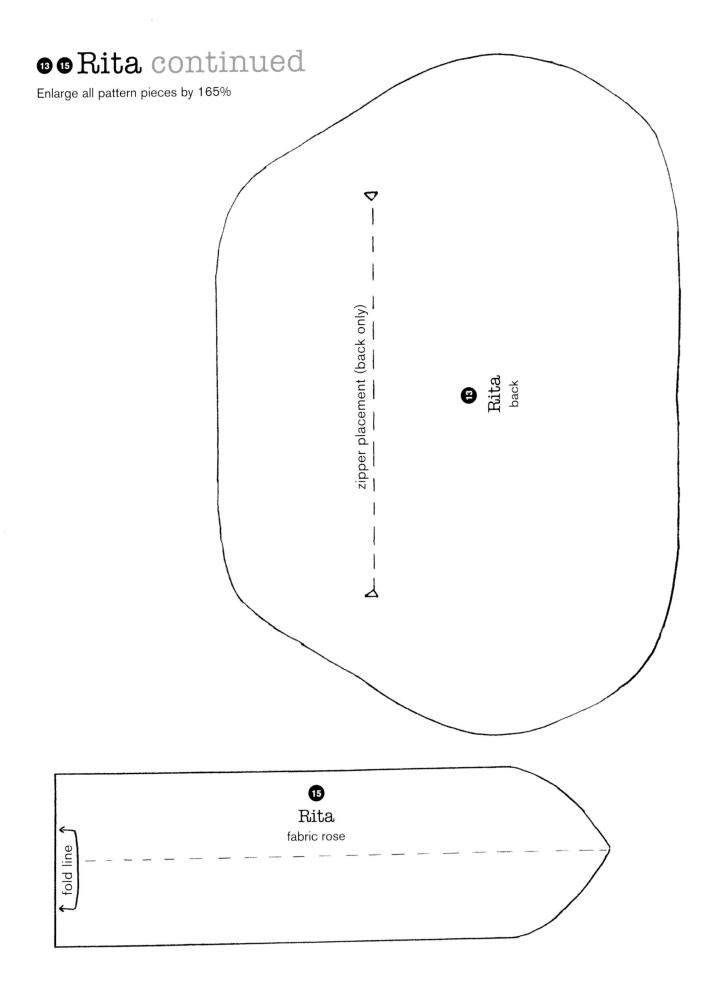

zipper placement (back only)

⓭ Rita
back

⓯
Rita
fabric rose

fold line

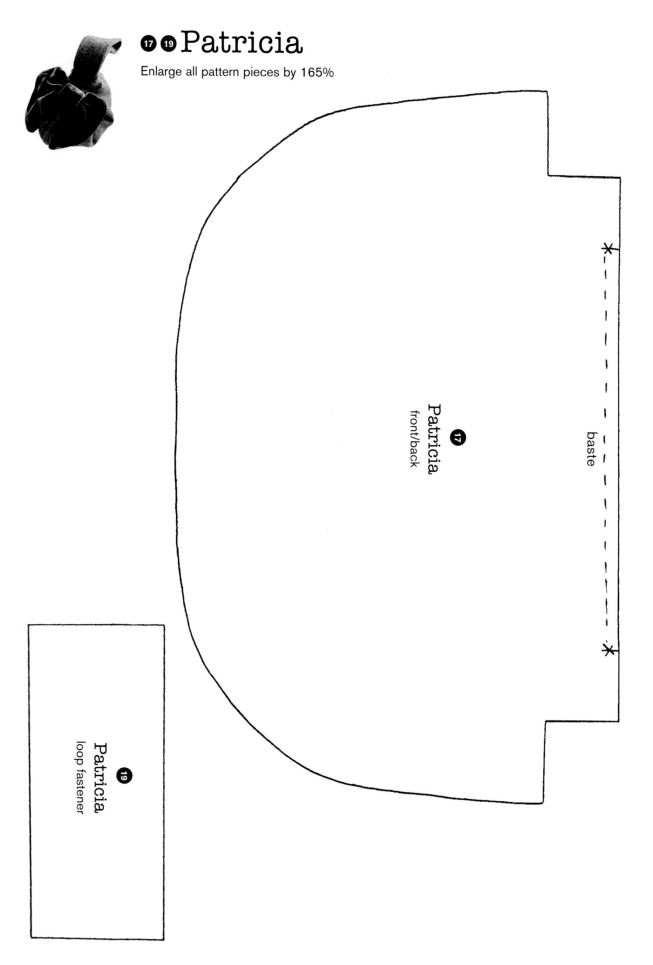

⑰ ⑲ Patricia

Enlarge all pattern pieces by 165%

Patricia
front/back
⑰

baste

Patricia
loop fastener
⑲

when photocopying, align dotted rule with top edge of glass

Enlarge all pattern pieces by 165%

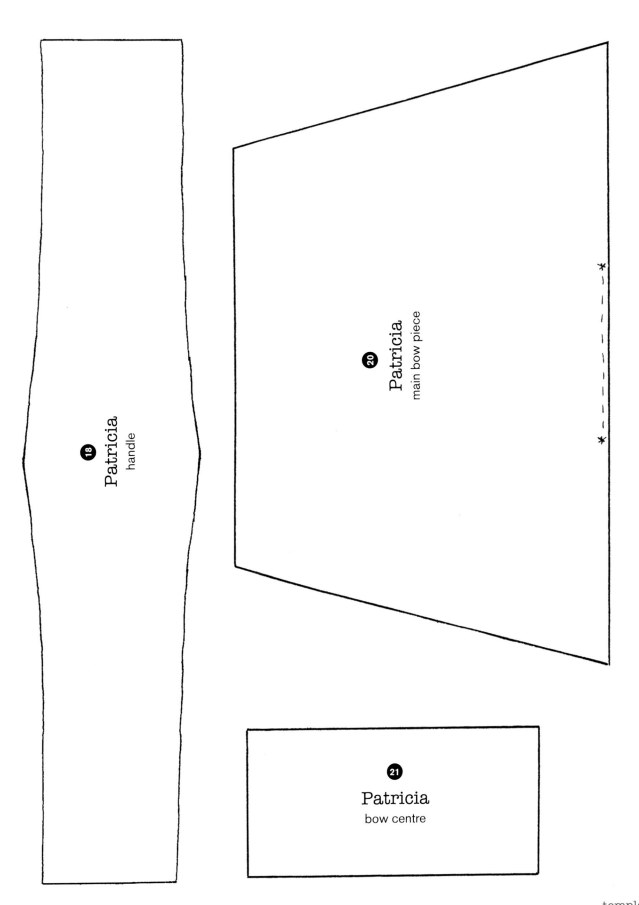

㉘ Patricia handle

⓴ Patricia main bow piece

㉑ Patricia bow centre

②② ②③ Shirley

Enlarge all pattern pieces by 165%

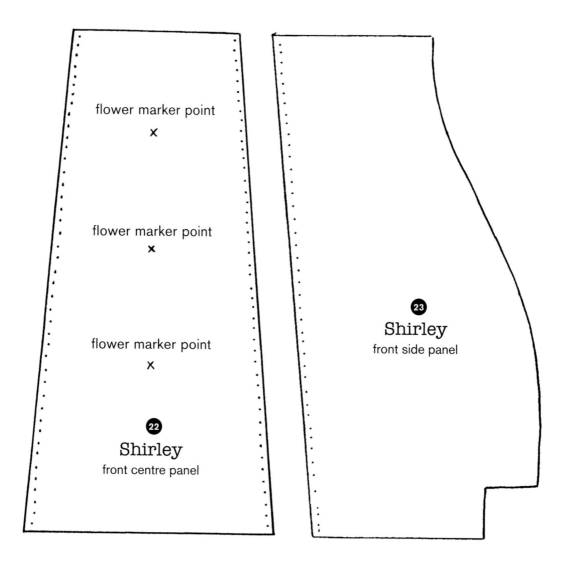

flower marker point
×

flower marker point
×

flower marker point
×

②②
Shirley
front centre panel

②③
Shirley
front side panel

Enlarge all pattern pieces by 165%

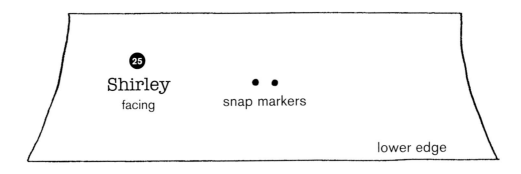

25
Shirley
facing

snap markers

lower edge

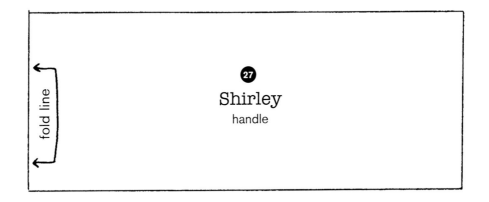

27
Shirley
handle

fold line

Enlarge all pattern pieces by 165%

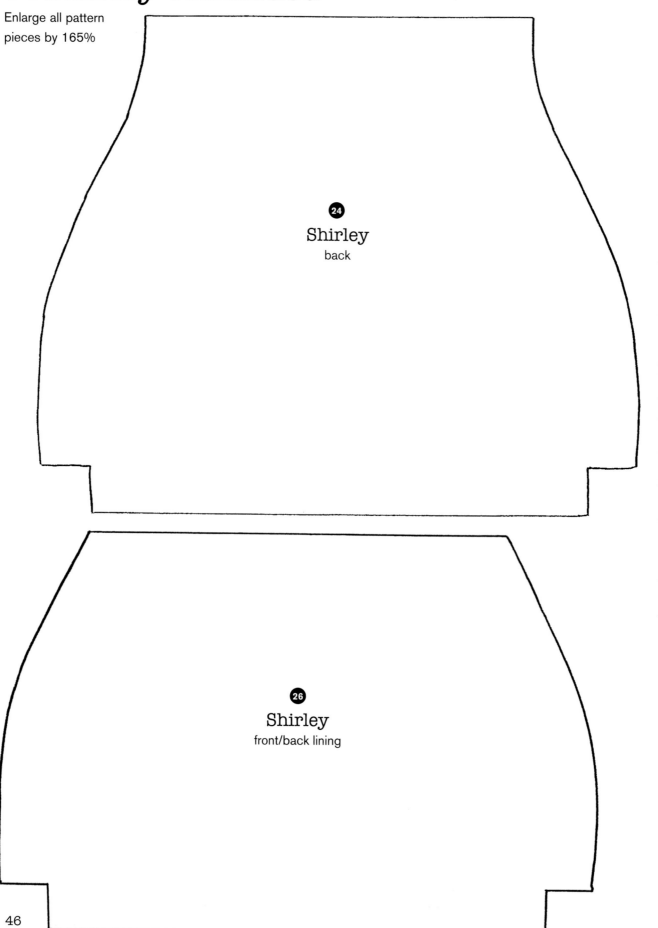

㉔
Shirley
back

㉖
Shirley
front/back lining

when photocopying, align dotted rule with top edge of glass

❷❾ Gloria

Enlarge all pattern pieces by 165%

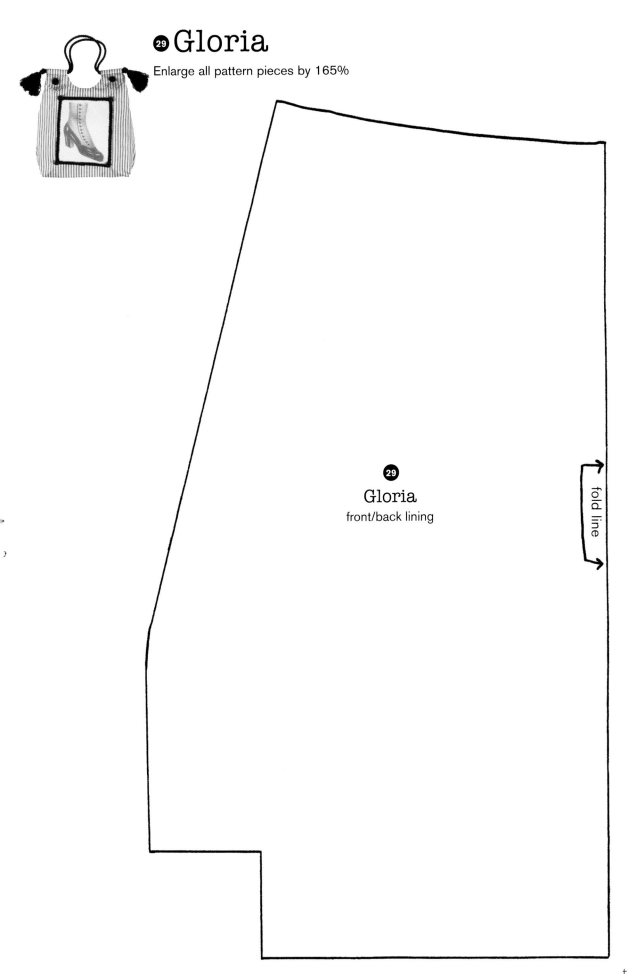

❷❾

Gloria
front/back lining

fold line

28 30 Gloria continued

Enlarge all pattern pieces by 165%

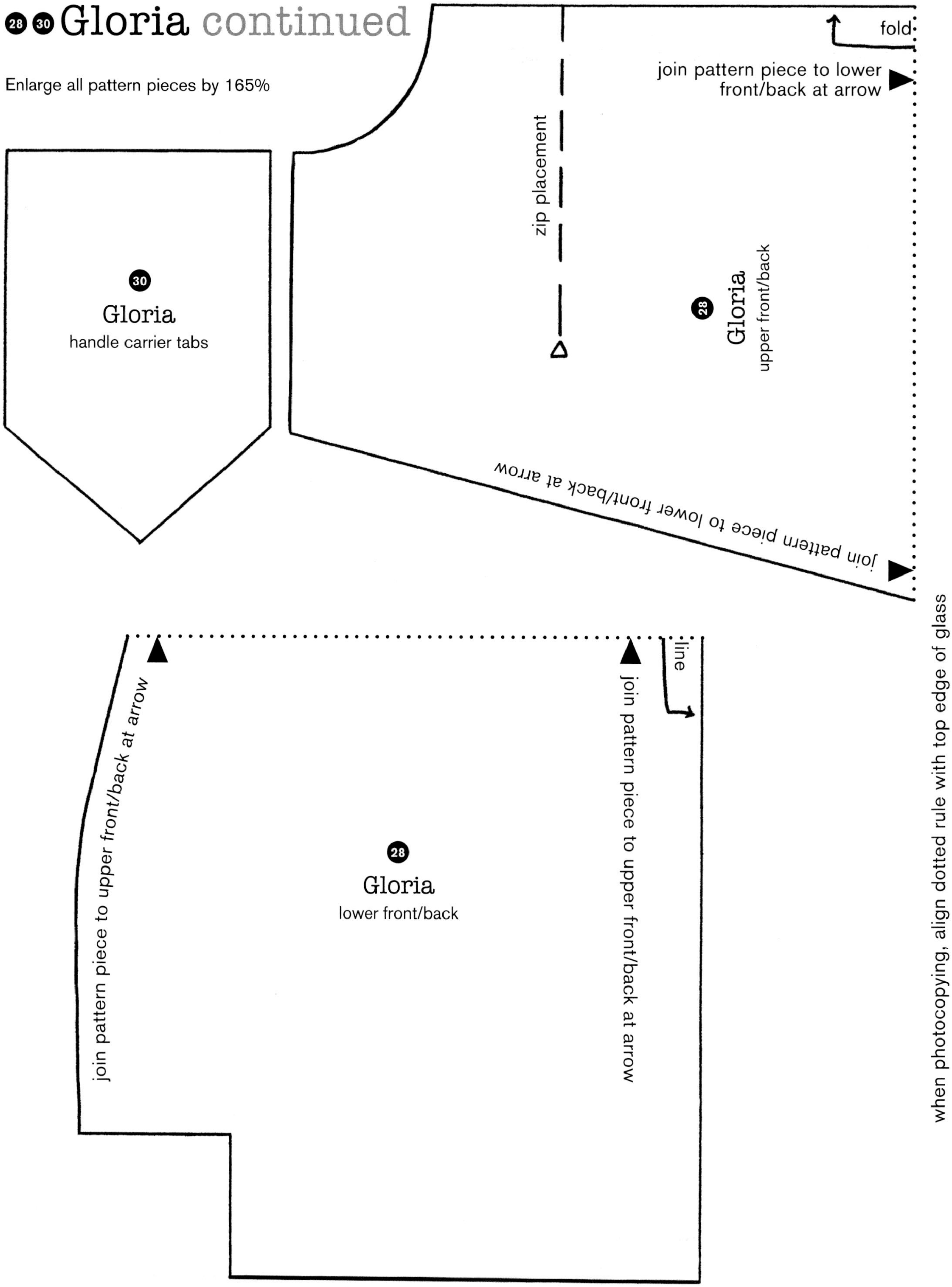

30
Gloria
handle carrier tabs
fold
join pattern piece to lower front/back at arrow
zip placement
28
Gloria
upper front/back
join pattern piece to lower front/back at arrow
line
join pattern piece to upper front/back at arrow
28
Gloria
lower front/back
join pattern piece to upper front/back at arrow
when photocopying, align dotted rule with top edge of glass